LEARNING TO BE HAPPY

LEARNING TO BE HAPPY

An easier-to-read and abridged version
of the classic *The Rare Jewel of Christian contentment,*
by Jeremiah Burroughs, first published in 1648.
The full work is available from the Banner of Truth
Trust

Rewritten for Grace Publications by Philip Tait from the
simplification prepared by Sharon James together with
questions for further thought.

Joint Managing Editors:
J. P. Arthur M.A.
H. J. Appleby

© GRACE PUBLICATIONS TRUST
175 Tower Bridge Road
London SE1 2AH
England
e-mail: AGBCSE@AOL.com

First published 1988
2nd Impression 1995
3rd Impresion 1998

ISBN 0 946462 16 X

Distributed by:
EVANGELICAL PRESS
Grange Close
Faverdale North
Darlington DL3 OPH
England

Printed in Great Britain by
Creative Print and Design (Wales), Ebbw Vale

Cover design: L.L. Evans

CONTENTS

* Jeremiah Burroughs has these two chapters in reverse order.

PREFACE

This book is about happiness. Not just any happiness, but the special kind of happiness that comes from being a Christian. We use various words to describe this happiness. I have generally called it "Christian happiness" or just "happiness"; but we must not think that this means being happy because we have everything we want. Another word we sometimes use is "joy"; but we must not think that this means wearing a big smile, even when we are in fact feeling sad. Another word for happiness is "contentment"; but we must not think that this means glumly accepting the will of God because there is nothing else we can do. What all these words describe is the deep inner satisfaction that Christians feel about what God has done for them. This inner satisfaction enables them to remain happy, and not to start complaining about God, even when things seem to be against them - just as a happy family remains a happy family even in times of sadness, because the members of the family are always satisfied with each other's company.

This book is a simplified and shorter version of "The Rare Jewel of Christian Contentment" by Jeremiah Burroughs (1599-1646). Burroughs' book is an exposition of Philippians 4:11. His method is to examine the subject of Christian contentment from various angles: he makes a large number of points, and often repeats what he has said in a different context. Some readers may therefore find it very confusing if they read this version of the book straight through: the best way to use it is to read and meditate on a little of it at a time.

I have kept strictly to the order in which Burroughs presents his points, except in the last two chapters, because I think it more logical to consider how to obtain happiness first, and then go on to how to keep it.

Philip Tait, Wembley, September 1987

1.
Christian Happiness

We all want to be happy, but we do not find it easy. The trouble is that we want to have everything this world offers, in the belief that this will make us happy. The apostle Paul had a quite different attitude. He wrote "I have learned to be content whatever the circumstances. I know what it is to be in need and I know what it is to have plenty. I have learned the secret of being content in any and every situation" (Philippians 4:11).

God is the only source of real happiness. He does not need anything or anyone to make him happy: even before he made the world, the three persons of the Trinity were completely happy with each other. What God does for Christians is to make them as happy as he is. This is necessary because they are not good enough or strong enough to make themselves happy. God gives them everything they need, as John wrote: "From the fulness of his grace we have all received one blessing after another" (John 1:16). So Christians can always be happy because even when they have very little of what this world offers, they have the spiritual blessings God gives us. In Christ they have everything they need.

This Christian happiness is sometimes called contentment. Paul wrote "Godliness with contentment is great gain. For we brought nothing into the world, and we can take nothing out of it. But if we have food and clothing, we will be content with that. People who want to get rich fall into temptation" (1 Timothy 6:6-9). "Keep your lives free from the love of money and be content with what you have, because God has said, 'Never will I leave you; never will I forsake you'." (Hebrews 13:5)

The first thing we can say about this Christian happiness is that it comes from within. It is possible to give the impression that because we are not complaining we are happy with what God has given us, when deep down we are still grumbling. But God sees what we are really thinking. David wrote "Find rest, O my soul, in God alone" (Psalm 62:5), because he knew that this was the only way he could be really happy. Similarly, this trust in God, this happiness that comes from within Christians, affects every part of them. David knew that God is in control of everything; but he could still become depressed, because he had not let this truth really affect the way he was thinking. That was why he wrote "Why are you downcast, O my soul? Why so disturbed within me?" (Psalm 42:5). Like him, we have to set our hearts on the kind of happiness that starts from within and makes us completely happy, like the heat of the body being trapped by thermal clothing and keeping us completely warm. And just as we stay warm once we have got warm under our winter clothes, so Christian happiness is something that goes on and on.

Another thing we can say about Christian happiness is that it is still there even when tragedies occur. When they are in trouble, Christians sorrow just like other people. When others are in trouble, Christians are sorry with them. They pray for themselves and for those who suffer, and this is worth doing because the Lord Jesus, who suffered when he was tempted, "is able to help those who are being tempted" (Hebrews 2:18). Though they pray to God, mature Christians who have problems do not grumble. When they are tempted to do so they control themselves. They do not complain about God, but go on obeying him and loving him. If they talk about their problems, they do so in prayer, because they still believe that God can help them.

A third important aspect of Christian happiness is the fact that it is the work of God. It is not the result of a naturally happy temperament, nor of a refusal to get involved with what is going on around them. Even non-Christians pull themselves together like that, and try not to worry. But Christian happiness is much more than "trying not to worry": it also has a positive element. The Christian wants to be happy all the time because that will glorify God.

So a fourth thing we can say about Christian happiness is that what makes a Christian really happy is doing what God wants. Christians are not forced to obey God. They do so willingly, and find that that makes them happy. When they stop to think, they realise that nothing makes them happy so much as submitting to God's will. They are content to let God plan for the future, even if his plans are quite different from what they intended. In fact they prefer his plans to their own, becuse they know that he knows what is good for them better than they do. After all, he understands them better than they understand themselves! Non-christians, who believe their fate is in their own hands, can only fear for the future, because one mistake could lead to disaster, whereas Christians have nothing to fear: they can commit the future to God, and then take pleasure in letting him guide them. Solomon wrote "Trust in the Lord with all your heart and lean not on your own understanding; in all your ways acknowledge him, and he will make your paths straight" (Proverbs 3:5,6,). Knowing that God is in control makes Christians happy both while they are experiencing trouble, and also afterwards, when they look back and see how God led them.

What is more, this Christian happiness lasts whatever kind of trouble is suffered. Christians do not have the right to decide what kind of suffering they will experience; to say, for example, that they are prepared to lose their possessions but not their health. They are happy whatever sort of suffering comes along. Perhaps one kind of suffering follows another, until their whole life seems to be made up of problems; but deep down they are still truly happy. Perhaps there seems to be no end in sight of their problems; but still, deep down, they are happy. And God, who has planned out their whole life for them, is glorified by that.

2.
The great secret

Paul wrote that he learned the secret of being content. He called it a secret because it is something that many people never learn, and because it is so difficult for non-christians to understand what it is that makes Christians happy. In this chapter we are going to consider some of the things about Christian happiness that can be really puzzling.

First of all, Christian happiness is puzzling because it involves being perfectly satisfied in one way, and completely dissatisfied in another. Christians are always happy to know that God is with them, but they are unhappy if they do not actually feel it. It also makes them unhappy when they remember what sinners they are, because it is sin that prevents them enjoying fellowship with God. Only in heaven will they be sinless and enjoy uninterrupted fellowship with God. In the meantime, they cannot be satisfied with the things that non-christians prefer. The sense of being loved by God is more important to them than anything the world offers. Asaph, who wrote several of the Psalms, felt like that, too. He wrote "Whom have I in heaven but you? And earth has nothing I desire besides you" (Psalm 73:25). And this feeling of being loved by God has kept Christians happy even in the most terrible troubles.

Christians also experience the peace which God gives, "which transcends all understanding" (Philippians 4:7). Having once experienced it, they cannot be happy without it, because they know it is the result of the Lord Jesus Christ, the Prince of Peace, being close to them. They experience peace when they are most obedient to him. Non-christians, on the other hand, want peace, but they do not want to obey the Lord Jesus. They should see that it is the Christians whom they meet who are most happy, satisfied, and peaceful people. And when they ask why this is so, the Christians should reply that it is because they are the servants of the Prince of Peace.

Again, Christian happiness is puzzling to the non-christian because it comes not from getting more but from wanting less. Non-christians think that the more they have to enjoy the happier they will be. Christians know that this will only make them happier for a short while: rich people are not necessarily happy people. But Christians find that what really makes them happy is wanting only the things that God chooses to give them. Their happiness arises not from the size of their bank balances, but from their willingness to be satisfied with what God gives them. A person who has many things but wants more will be miserable. A person who has a few things but does not want anything else will be happy, just as someone with two short legs walks far more comfortably than someone with one long leg and one short one! This is a most important lesson for Christians to learn in days like these, when non-christians are always wanting - and getting - more and more material things. Christians need to show others how to be happy by wanting less rather than by having more.

A third puzzling thing about Christian happiness is that sometimes the way to be happy is not to stop worrying, but to start worrying about something else. Suppose we are unhappy about some problem that is affecting us. We are deceiving ourselves if we think that all we need to make us happy is to take away the problem. The thing that is really making us unhappy is sin. If we worried more about that, our other problems would not seem so great. A particular sin that Christians are liable to commit is to forget that everything they have comes from God, and they forget to thank him, or they start to blame God for the things they are suffering. If they remembered that God is always better to them than they deserve, they would find it easier to be happy, even in times of trouble. For example, if a family find their plans for the future are not working out as they intended, they may be tempted to start quarrelling and blaming each other; but quarrelling is a sin, and they must stop it and ask God to forgive them if they want to be happy in the future.

Another thing about Christian happiness that can be really puzzling is that a problem does not have to be removed before we can be happy. Sometimes God blesses us while we are suffering. Paul wrote "The sinful nature desires what is contrary to the Spirit, and the Spirit what is contrary to the sinful nature. They are in conflict with each other, so that you do not do what you want" (Galatians 5:17). This struggle is going on within every Christian all of the time. Sometimes a problem helps us to triumph over the sinful nature and draw closer to God, and in that way suffering becomes a blessing.

A fifth puzzling thing about Christian happiness is that it is achieved not by wanting more or having more but by doing more. The Christian says "God is behind what has happened to me, and it is his doing that I am not as happy as I once was. But I must not complain. I must look for new ways of serving God, and finding happiness in obeying him." Christians will be happier by serving God where they are, and not by stretching out for what they do not have, like children trying to touch the clouds.

A sixth thing making Christian happiness puzzling to non-christians is that what makes Christians happy is learning to accept that God's will is best. When they learn that, they do not worry that they cannot have exactly what they want; indeed they are happy to want what God wants, to love what he loves, to hate what he hates. They say "God has made me spiritually wise; God has made me holy; God has taught me to accept that his will is best. And because he is satisfied with that and glorified by that, I am happy."

We can sum up these six puzzling things by saying that what makes the Christian happy is the fact that God is making him holy, and his happiness therefore depends on what God is doing. When James wrote "What causes fights and quarrels among you? Don't they come from your desires and battles within you?" he was showing that what causes unhappiness between Christians is sin in their lives. If we get rid of those inner, sinful feelings that lead to ungodliness we shall be much happier. In short, true happiness is not the result of what we have but of the kind of people we are. This is the great secret of happiness.

Now those who are happy like this, happy within because godly within, find they are pleased with whatever God sends them. For Christians know that everything they have is a gift from God - health, home, food, clothes, friends, family, employment, opportunities, entertainments. Every one of them is a gift from God, a token of his love. So Christians are pleased with them all, and happy to receive them. They may have less than some non-christians, but they appreciate more what they have, because they know it is better to have a little and be a child of God than to have a lot and be under his condemnation. What is more, Christians know that every token of God's love they receive is like a deposit or a guarantee that in the life to come God will give them all the good things he has promised. Everything he gives them makes them happy and serves to remind them how much happier they will be in heaven.

Again, believers who are happy within because godly within, find that when they suffer they get more comfort from thinking about the Lord Jesus than they ever could from complaining. They read the New Testament and see how much the Lord Jesus suffered, and they know that the Lord feels for them when they suffer because he knows what it is like to suffer. The Lord Jesus has experienced every physical, material, emotional and spiritual agony. For example, he was poor, so he can comfort Christians who are poor; he was abused, so he can comfort Christians who are the victims of injustice; he was tortured, so he can comfort Christians who ask him for strength in suffering. The Lord has promised "When you pass through the waters, I will be with you." Christians may be frightened of dying, but they are encouraged when they think about the death of the Lord Jesus, and especially when they remember that he rose from death.

This is the only way Christians can get strength when they suffer. They turn to Christ, who has the power to forgive their sins, to make them holy, and to help them in all their trials. Writing to some Christians who were having to endure great trials, Paul told them that they would have to depend not on their own resources but on the strength that Christ gives. His prayer was that they would be "strengthened with all power according to his glorious might." This was so that they might have "great endurance and patience" (Colossians 1:11).

Finally, whoever is happy within because godly within, finds that the greatest happiness of all comes from knowing God. The writer of Lamentations had everything to depress him, as the city of Jerusalem had just been taken by an enemy, and it seemed that there was no future for the people of God. But he knew that the only real source of happiness was God himself, so he wrote "The Lord is my portion; therefore I will wait for him" (Lamentations 3:24). We have seen that God gives Christians everything they have. The things he gives bring happiness, just as pipes bring water. But sometimes the supply is cut off, and water has to be taken directly from the well. In just the same way, when the things God gives are not there any longer, we have to go to the source of happiness, to God himself. As time goes by, Christians find increasingly that the source of real happiness is God himself. In heaven he will be the only source of happiness: "I did not see a temple in the city, because the Lord God Almighty and the Lamb are its temple. The city does not need the sun or the moon to shine on it, for the glory of God is its light, and the Lamb is its lamp" (Revelation 21:22,23). Even here on earth, we can begin to experience this happiness in God alone.

The Lord Jesus sums up the things we have learnt in this chapter: "The kingdom of God does not come with your careful observation, nor will people say, 'Here it is', or 'There it is', because the kingdom of God is within you" (Luke 17:20-21). Christians look forward to being in heaven, but in a sense they have the enjoyment of heaven already. They know that having experienced a taste of heaven in this life, they will experience it in full in heaven. In the meantime, everything they experience of God satisfies them completely, for they have no needs which Christ cannot meet.

But this kind of happiness comes only when there is peace within a person, like a happy family in which there is peace within the home. The non-christian is not at peace and so cannot be happy, like a family which is unhappy because they are always quarrelling.

Christians know that the fact that they have this peace and happiness within them is an indication that they will enjoy the peace and happiness of heaven. Knowing this enabled some Christians bravely to die rather than deny the faith, as they looked forward to being in heaven. The apostle Paul wrote "We do not lose heart. Though outwardly we are wasting away, yet inwardly we are being renewed day by day. For our light and momentary troubles are achieving for us an eternal glory that far outweighs them all. So we fix our eyes not on what is seen, but what is unseen. For what is seen is temporary, but what is unseen is eternal" (2 Corinthians 4:16-18). In the next chapter we will consider why Christians can be sure that God will do what he has promised.

Questions to help you think about chapters 1 and 2

1. What are the greatest causes of discontent in your life?.. be honest!

2. Contentment is part of the character of God himself and is a precious gift which he gives to his children. What do you understand to be the nature of this contentment?

3. Chapter 2 speaks about Christian contentment as a great secret - something that cannot be understood by the person who is not a Christian. If we are honest, we surely have to admit that many Christians are ignorant of this secret. Why is this so?

4. What is, or ought to be, the relationship between Christian contentment and the promise of glory to come?

5. "Christian happiness .... comes not from getting more but from wanting less". How can we keep our wants in check?

6. As Christians, how are our wants and expectations different from those of our non-christian relatives, friends and neighbours?

7. What is the relationship between contentment and godliness?

8. In the light of your answers to the questions above, what changes are needed in your life and attitude?

3.
The promises of God

God has made great promises to all who believe in Jesus Christ. Thinking about the certainty of what God has promised helps to make Christians happy.

God, who is righteous, cannot ignore sin. But he is also a loving God, who felt pity for sinners: he wanted to save them from the punishment they deserved, and because they could not help themselves, he decided to help them, and to be merciful to some and save them. So he sent his Son, the Lord Jesus Christ, who agreed to become a man and live a life of perfect obedience to God, his Father; his obedience is credited to the people of God. The Lord Jesus was put to death by being crucified; the Lord Jesus was taking on himself the punishment the people of God deserve for their sin. So we can say that God has promised to credit Christ's obedience to believers, to take their guilt from them by laying it on Christ, and to give them eternal life. The Holy Spirit gives new life to them. He brings them to believe on the Lord Jesus

Christ, gives them assurance of salvation, and strengthens them so that they can overcome the influence of sin.

God's promises are the result of his grace; that is, they are given to those who do not deserve them. And the things that God promises to give are for all eternity: the death of Christ has obtained the certain and everlasting salvation of his people, and he will not let them be lost. The promises are given to Christians as individuals, and the things God promises are given to them personally.

The promises God has given are a great encouragement to Christians. He has promised to save all his people, which gives them a feeling of security and makes them very happy. He has promised that the devil will never overcome them, and this also gives them a feeling of security, even when they face troubles and disappointments. Even when the future is uncertain, they are happy because they know that God's promises are unbreakable. David had total confidence in the faithfulness of God, and knew that he would keep his word: "Is not my house right with God? Has he not made with me an everlasting covenant arranged and secured in every part? Will he not bring to fruition my salvation and grant me my every desire?" (2 Samuel 23:5). And Christians today have even more reason than David to be sure that God will keep his word. They look at the work of the Lord Jesus, who has brought them everything that God promised. In the Old Testament the people of Israel could rejoice because God had promised to be good to the nation: but Christians today can rejoice in the better things that God has done for them as individuals (Hebrews 8).

Besides the promise of salvation, God has made many other wonderful promises. All these promises must be understood in the light of the great promises God has made about salvation, for it is not helpful to think that literal interpretations exhaust the meaning of such promises. For example, Psalm 91 contains promises that the man of God will not suffer illness, accident or harm. Christians who face suffering may wonder if this psalm has anything to say to them. It may be the people of Israel were entitled to expect physical and external blessings in return for obedience; certainly the blessings promised and the curses threatened in the law of Moses suggest that this was the case. But the promise of verses 9 and 10 "If you make the Most High your dwelling - even the Lord, who is my refuge - then no harm will befall you, no disaster will come near your tent", should not be taken to mean that Christians will never suffer. Rather, it teaches them to have confidence that God is watching over them at all times and guarding them from evil. He may use hardship to discipline them, just as a father punishes his children : this proves that they are the children of God. He has the right to give them whatever he sees fit, and to take away whatever he sees fit; but it is always for their good. If something occurs that seems to be harming them, they can be certain that it is all part of God's plans for their good. So no real harm, no spiritual harm, no eternal harm can befall them.

Among the Old Testament promises that Christians can apply to themselves are Isaiah 43:2 and Joshua 1:5. The writer to the Hebrews quotes the promise from Joshua in a very strong way, as if God were saying "No, I will not leave you: I will not, no, I will not" (Hebrews 13:5).

So God has made these promises and many others like them. All the promises point to heaven, and teach us that some of the pleasure of being in heaven can be enjoyed here and now, as sailors on a stormy sea are comforted by thinking of the shore.

4.
The school of happiness

In this chapter we are going to school, but not to study mathematics, science or geography. Christ is the teacher, and he will teach us how to be happy. There are ten lessons. Christians who work through this course will find they can be really happy whatever happens to them. And remember - not only is Christ the teacher, but his life is the perfect example of happiness in all circumstances.

Lesson 1 - Deny yourself!

Being a Christian is costly. Christians who pretend otherwise are not telling the truth. Jesus was quite blunt about this: he said "If anyone would come after me, he must deny himself and take up his cross daily and follow me. For whoever wants to save his life will lose it, but whoever loses his life for me will save it" (Luke 9:23,24). It is Christ himself who teaches Christians how to deny themselves. He teaches them that they are unworthy of God's attention, that they deserve nothing but God's anger against their sin, that they can do nothing without his help: they realise, when things they enjoy are taken from them, that they are not entitled to anything from God because they do so little for him. Christ teaches them that they are so sinful they are likely to spoil the good things he gives them, and though he may bless them and enable them to use these things well, if he leaves them alone they are sure to misuse them. He teaches them that if they die their work will not collapse; God can easily appoint someone else to take it over. Understanding these things is what is meant by denying ourselves. We should try hard to realise how unimportant we are. Then every trouble will seem small and every blessing great.

Lesson 2 - Christ's self-denial

No-one ever denied himself like Christ. Isaiah wrote "He was oppressed and afflicted, yet he did not open his mouth; he was led like a lamb to the slaughter, and as a sheep before her shearers is dumb, so he did not open his mouth" (Isaiah 53:7). Isaiah was prophesying how Christ would submit to death as a sacrifice for the sins of his people. Paul wrote about him that he "made himself nothing, taking the very nature of a servant, being made in human likeness. And being found in appearance as a man, he humbled himself and became obedient to death

- even death on a cross!" (Philippians 2:7,8). And yet he was the most contented person who ever lived. The closer Christians come to following his example of self-denial, the happier they will be. Christ rejoiced in doing his Father's will; and Christians need to learn that whereas selfish people can only be happy when God does what they want, self-denying people are happy with whatever God does.

Lesson 3 - Nothing satisfies without God

"Everything is meaningless" says the Preacher. "What does man gain from all his labour at which he toils under the sun?" (Ecclesiastes 1:2,3). Those who are unhappy with the things this world provides are not, as they tend to think, unhappy because they do not have enough, but because the things of this world simply cannot bring happiness. Mankind was made to know and enjoy God. The great theologian Augustine wrote "You made us for yourself, and our hearts are restless until they rest in you." Unhappy people who think that having more things will satisfy them are like starving people thinking that mouthfuls of air will stop the pangs of their hunger. "Why spend money on what is not bread, and your labour on what does not satisfy?" (Isaiah 55:2). Nothing is worth having without God.

Lesson 4 - Christ satisfies

Jesus Christ taught that he himself makes people really happy. He said "I am the living bread that came down from heaven. If anyone eats of this bread, he will live for ever" (John 6:51). He also said "If anyone is thirsty, let him come to me and drink. Whoever believes in me, as the Scripture has said, streams of living water will flow from within him" (John 7:37). Bread and water are the most basic needs of our bodies. Jesus was teaching that he satisfies the most basic needs of our souls, just as Isaiah had prophesied: "Listen, listen to me, and eat what is good, and your soul will delight in the richest of fare" (Isaiah 55:2). Jesus promised that his people would have "life, and have it to the full", and that their joy would be complete (John 10:10; 16:24).

Lesson 5 - Be a traveller and a fighter!

Christians are travellers. They are just passing through this world, just camping in their bodies. They are preparing for an eternity in heaven when God will give them perfect resurrection bodies. So it is foolish to get too unhappy about the state of our present bodies. The people we read about in Hebrews 11 "admitted they were aliens and strangers on earth ...... they were longing for a better country - a heavenly one. Therefore God is not ashamed to be called their God, for he has prepared a city for them" (verses 13,16). Christians must learn to think like this. Travellers who are away from home accept some inconveniences, such as poor food, or difficult travelling conditions. Christians have an eternal home, and the inconvenience of their stay on earth should not worry them unduly.

Christians are also fighters. Paul wrote to Timothy "Endure hardship with us like a good soldier of Christ Jesus" (2 Timothy 2:3). A soldier who is away from home, on an exercise or on active service, does not expect home comforts. Christians are soldiers, fighting the devil, the enemy of their souls. They must be willing to put up with hardship. They must remember that the Christian life is one long battle, and there are bound to be hardships. But whereas a soldier cannot know who will win the war in the end, Christians can be certain that Jesus Christ will see to it that victory is theirs at last.

Lesson 6 - Enjoy the good times

The whole of God's world is here for men and women to enjoy. They can be really happy, knowing that everything they have comes from God, and being thankful to him. Christians look at the things God has made, and they see that he is good. So the things he has made make them happy. But they have to realise that their possessions are not the most important of the things God has given them, and that they may have to make do without them if that is what God wants. God may call on them to serve him in difficult times; or he may call on them to serve him in good times, and if he does, he means them to enjoy the good things he gives. But he will choose what is best for them, and they must learn to be happy with that. An employee who refuses to move to another job when asked to do so by the manager will not please the management!

Lesson 7 - Know yourself!

All Christians should study themselves, and find out what their deepest desires are. This will teach them that it is not the circumstances of their lives that make them unhappy, but the state of their hearts. The real cause of unhappiness is often sin. Christians who know themselves can nip sin in the bud and save themselves a lot of unhappiness.

Christians who do not know themselves will very probably become very fearful when problems arise. They will begin to say "Perhaps God has forgotten me!" But if they know that they need to be humbled, they will understand that God sends troubles to test them or to discipline them. A drug with unpleasant side-effects may save your life, and an experience which involves some unpleasantness may keep you from sin.

As the Christian grows in self-knowledge his prayers improve. Immature Christians who do not understand their own hearts pray for unhelpful things, and then become depressed because they do not get everything they want.

Lesson 8 - Beware of riches!

Christians often envy those who are rich, and fail to see the problems riches bring. "For the love of money is a root of all kinds of evil. Some people, eager for money, have wandered from the faith and pierced themselves with many griefs" (1 Timothy 6:10). A new pair of shoes may look good, but the wearer knows how they pinch; a city may appear beautiful, but the inhabitants know the squalor of the slums; and the people may be rich and prosperous on the outside, but sorrowful on the inside.

People who are rich or famous often face sorrows and problems. Prosperity can bring trouble. Prosperity can bring temptation: Jesus said it was very hard for rich people to enter the kingdom of heaven. What is more, rich and notable people will one day have to give an account to God of how they used their riches or their fame.

Lesson 9 - Beware of getting what you want!

Several places in the Bible tell us about people getting what they want. What people want is often selfish, and it would do them no good to have it; so when God gives them what they want it is a severe punishment. "But my people would not listen to me; Israel would not submit to me. So I gave them over to their stubborn hearts to follow their own devices" (Psalm 81:11,12). Bernard

(1090-1153) who was Abbot of Clairvaux, said "Do not let me have such a misery as that; for to give me what I want to have, to give me what my heart desires, is one of the most awful judgements in the world." Learning that our natural desires can so lead us astray is one of the hardest but one of the most important lessons in the school of Christ.

Lesson 10 - God is in control!

God rules the whole universe, and that means that even the smallest details of what happens are under his control. So everything that happens to Christians happens because that is God's will for them, and because he sees that it will be good for them. Jesus encouraged his disciples by reminding them of this. He said "Are not five sparrows sold for two pennies? Yet not one of them is forgotten by God. Indeed, the very hairs of your head are all numbered. Don't be afraid; you are worth more than many sparrows" (Luke 12:6,7).

Christians should pray that God will increase their faith so that they can appreciate his care in planning everything that happens to them. They should remember that they simply cannot understand all that God is doing with them. For all they know, God has a purpose to fulfil in their lives in twenty years' time which depends on something that is happening this week. If they resist his will for this week, they are resisting his will for all the other things that depend on this week.

God works in various ways, and it helps Christians to be happy with what God does when they understand a little about the way God works. There are two things in particular that they can learn about God's way of working.

First, it is normal for the people of God to suffer. Nonchristians think that if there really is a God, and if these people really belong to him, then they would not suffer. But the reverse is true: the fact that they suffer proves they belong to Christ. Peter wrote "Dear friends, do not be surprised at the painful trial you are suffering, as though something strange were happening to you. But rejoice that you participate in the sufferings of Christ, so that you may be overjoyed when his glory is revealed" (1 Peter 4:12,13).

Second, God can bring great good out of great evil. Often God brings his people through great trials before being especially good to them. Joseph was a prisoner before he became the governor of Egypt; David was on the run before he became King of Israel; and Jesus Christ himself suffered and died before he was raised from death and glorified. Luther said "It is God's way; he humbles so that he may raise up; he kills so that he may make alive; he overcomes so that he may glorify."

5.
Happiness is good for you

Happiness is good for you. In this chapter we are going to consider why a happy Christian is a blessed Christian.

First of all, happy Christians worship God as he ought to be worshipped. True worship is not just attending services and saying our prayers. On the contrary, it is possible to go through an act of worship, but with such a discontented heart that we have not really worshipped God at all. God wants Christians to worship him with all they have and all they are. Then, and only then, do they truly please him and really worship him. To do what God wants, that is worship; to be pleased with what God gives, that too is worship. Worship and happiness go together.

Second, happy Christians are those who make best use of the spiritual gifts God gives them, such as faith, humility, love, patience, wisdom and hope. God wants to see these things develop in his people, because the lives of happy Christians are often a helpful influence on non-christians. For example, people who suffer without complaining are unusual: Christians who do so give a good testimony which gives glory to God.

So the third thing we can say is that happy Christians glorify God. Nature glorifies God, because he made it; and Christians who remain happy despite their trials glorify him because he made them like that. When unbelievers see believers happy in times of trouble, they are convinced that God is at work.

Again, happy Christians are those to whom God is most gracious. If they want God to be good to them, they must remain quietly happy. They must not behave like spoilt children, who shout and scream until they get what they want. Wise parents will let the child scream and give him nothing until he quietens down. Christians who pray for something and then become angry because they do not get it immediately often find that God waits until they are quiet and submissive before he gives them what they need. A prisoner in chains will only be bruised by angry struggling. He must be still to allow anyone to free him.

Again, happy Christians are the most useful Christians. Unstable, restless people are not fit to serve God. Only when God by his Spirit has calmed them down will they be ready to work for him. And all Christians are called to work for God, not just the leaders or those with special training. They should not think that because they are only ordinary people they are no use to God, or that only the things that are done publicly really constitute serving God. The only thing that fits them for serving

God is an inner spiritual contentment.

Sixth, happy Christians are better equipped to resist temptation. People who grumble are easily led astray. The devil loves Christians to be anxious, and when they face suffering he does his best to persuade them that it is not fair; then they become convinced that this should not be happening to them. Or he may tempt poor Christians to steal or wronged Christians to take revenge. Those who are happy with what God sends are proof against such temptations.

Seventh, happy Christians are those who enjoy life here and now to the full. Sometimes people who have few possessions are happier than those who have many, because they have learned how to be satisfied with what they have, just as a nation that is content with the territory it occupies is happier than one that is continually going to war.

Finally, happy Christians are those who look forward to the rewards God promises. God rewards everyone for their deeds. God will reward Christians for their good deeds, and even for those good intentions they were unable to put into effect. He will reward evil people for their wicked deeds, including the wicked plans they made but were restrained from carrying out. So Christians who suffer for Christ's sake without becoming embittered by the experience can be sure that they will not lose their reward.

Questions to help you think about chapters 3-5

1. How has what you have read and thought about thus far affected your life and attitudes?

2. Chapter 3 suggested that the promises of God ought to make the Christian happy or content. Have there been times when you have felt unhappy because God has seemed not to keep some of his promises?
Look at Psalm 91. How should we treat such promises as these? How should we cope with situations where God does not seem to deal with us according to the promises of his Word?

3. Chapter 4 suggests that one of the ways in which we can guard ourselves against a spirit of discontent is by having a right estimate of ourselves - not having too high an opinion of ourselves and of what we deserve. How important is self-image to Christian happiness?

4. How is a practical appreciation of the sovereignty of God a necessary ingredient in Christian contentment?

5. Jesus speaks of his ability to satisfy the thirsty (see John 4:13,14). The one who has Christ should be content with him. What does this mean in practical terms?

6. Chapter 4 suggests that Christians need to learn to be content. If the church is the school in which we are learning of Christ, in what ways can we help one another with our lessons?

6.
Complaining is bad for you

In the first five chapters of this book, we have looked at Christian happiness in various ways, so that we could learn what it is and why it is so important. In the second half of the book, we are going to learn something about how to live happy Christian lives. The opposite of happiness is a bitter, complaining spirit that sees the worst side of everything. In this chapter we are going to consider what is wrong with complaining, and we shall discover that it is both sinful and unhelpful. In chapter 7 we shall look at some situations in which complaining is particularly serious, and in chapter 8 we shall consider some of the common excuses we make for complaining. Then we will be ready to see how to get happiness and how to stay happy.

Complaining is bad for us, first of all, because once we start, it only gets worse. A complaining spirit is like a bad wound that has gone septic. The infected flesh cannot be treated; it must be cut away, or the infection will spread through the whole body. And a tendency to complain, if it is not checked, will spread through the whole of our lives and blight everything.

Why is complaining so serious? Because - and this is the second thing we can say about it - complaining is sinful. In Jude 14-16, "grumblers" are placed first in the list of the ungodly whom God will judge. Complaining is sinful: God will judge those who do it. What a serious thought!

But why is complaining sinful? The third thing that we can say about complaining is that it involves rebellion against God. When the Israelites were in the desert they complained over and over again. God had rescued them from slavery in Egypt, but they were not happy and grateful for very long. And every time they complained, God regarded the complaint as directed against himself (Numbers 14:26-29). In Numbers 16 the people complained about Moses and Aaron, but God treated that as a complaint against himself, and a terrible punishment broke out against the rebels: complaining is serious, and it must be dealt with before the complaining spirit spreads to others.

But, fourth, for the people of God to complain is especially serious because it is a contradiction of everything that happened when God converted them. He made them see their sin and admit their guilt: and can they really let less important things make them unhappy? He showed them Christ's wonderful love, willingness to leave his Father and the glories of heaven, patience in accepting the limitations of a human body, humble submission, perfect life, and sinless death. Can they really forget all that, and complain that God has not been good to them? He freed them from the need to have material things to make them happy: and are they really going to complain because of that? Christ is now their Lord and King: are they really going to reject his leadership by complaining about him? God brought them to submit to his will: and if they now complain, it suggests they never really submitted, and perhaps they are not Christians at all. If Christians remember what God has done for them, his love, his forgiveness, his gift of new life, and if they remember that he converted them precisely so that they could live in the light of all those things until their dying day, they will not complain, but will want to submit to Jesus Christ as their Lord and King and Saviour.

The fifth thing that we can say about complaining is that it is below the standard that God sets for Christians. God is their Father: if they complain, it implies that they do not believe he is willing or able to look after their best interests. Christ is their husband: if they complain it implies that they mistrust his love. The Holy Spirit is their helper: if they complain, it implies they do not really believe that he can or will help them.

Let us look in more detail at the standards God sets for Christians. He has raised them to a position of great honour, made them lords of heaven and earth, brought them nearer to himself than even the angels, united them with Christ; Christians are in a position of great privilege. But God had a purpose in calling them to that position. It was so that their lives should show the power of God. God has a right to expect that those whom he has honoured so greatly will not complain.

God is not only their Saviour: he is also their Father. Fathers love to see their own good points coming out in their children, and God loves to see his Spirit at work in his children. He especially wants to see them becoming like his Son Jesus Christ, who suffered greatly and never once complained, but prayed "Not what I will, but what you will." God has a right to expect that his children will not complain.

If Christians claim that God means more to them than the things of this world, they should prove it by the way they live. It is better not to claim to be a Christian, than to be inconsistent in behaviour. God has a right to expect that those who claim to be Christians will keep up to Christian standards.

God has given Christians faith, so that they are sure that everything he has promised is theirs by right. The Bible says they should "live by faith". This does not mean that they can expect everything to be trouble-free. If that were true, there would be no need of faith! What it does mean is that they can cheerfully accept God's will, because they know that he has promised all sorts of good things to them. And God has a right to expect that those who have been taught to believe his promises will not complain.

In short, God expects Christians to be patient in times of trial and to rejoice in times of difficulty. By his grace many have already attained this high standard: we can read about some of them in Hebrews 11, ordinary people who depended on God to support them when the going was hard. God expects it; others have done it; so can we!

Returning now to the subject of complaining, a sixth thing we must note is that complaining makes a nonsense of our prayers. We cannot say "Your will be done", and expect our will to be done! We cannot say "Give us today our daily bread", and expect luxuries for tomorrow! The very act of praying means that we acknowledge that everything we have comes from God. If we are going to start complaining about what God gives, we may as well give up praying.

Seventh, complaining only causes unhappiness. It is a waste of time: our minds become so much taken up with complaints that we stop thinking about God and the Word of God. It makes us useless for the service of God: a happy person can offer comfort to others in their time of need, but a complainer has nothing to give. Complaining is the first step to running away from God, and like Jonah, attempting to frustrate God's will rather than submit to it. Worst of all, complaining makes us ungrateful, and the Bible regards ingratitude as a sin. Complaining Christians are not thankful for all the many gifts they have; they claim they want greater gifts so that they can glorify God all the more, but they are not really grateful for what they already have. Christians can be ungrateful like this both with the spiritual gifts God gives them and with the material blessings they have. But God expects Christians to be thankful, and to praise him for all he has given them. Luther said "The method of the Spirit of God is to think less about evil things and more about good things: to think that if a cross comes, it is but a little one, but that if a mercy comes, it is a great one." If a trial comes, Christians should thank God that it is not as severe as it might be. The Holy Spirit teaches them how to make much of their blessings and little of their problems. The devil does the opposite: look at the Israelites in the desert. They said to Moses "Isn't it enough that you have brought us up out of a land flowing with milk and honey to kill us in the desert? And now you also want to lord it over us?" (Numbers 16:13). The complaining spirit had got into them to such an extent that they were distorting the truth. Egypt, the land of slavery, forced labour, beatings, and the slaughter of their children was not a "land flowing with milk and honey"; Moses' leadership was being called into question, and his motives misrepresented. Christians can behave like this too: when problems come, they are tempted to think they were happier before, and that thought only makes them still unhappier.

So we can add an eighth thing about complaining. Since all that it does is to make us unhappier it is not only sinful but also foolish. What is the use of complaining about what we do not have? Does it make it easier to enjoy the things we do have? Is a child who throws away his bread because there is no cake going to satisfy his hunger? Complaining is useless: "Who of you" says the Lord Jesus "by worrying can add a single hour to his life?" (Matthew 6:27). The answer, of course, is that no-one can! People may worry themselves to death, but complaining will do them no good. God may withhold a blessing until they are in a suitable state of mind to receive it. Or if God grants the blessing, Christians may find that their spirits are now so embittered that they cannot appreciate the goodness of God. The fact of the matter is that complaining is foolish because it makes things worse. Complaining Christians are proud Christians, who refuse to submit to God's will for them. They are like sailors who complain about a storm instead of preparing their ship to meet it. Sensible sailors bow to the storm and pull down the sails.

The last two things we may note about complaining are very serious. Complaining provokes the anger of God. He was angry when the Israelites complained: he is angry when Christians complain. The Israelites were punished because they complained; and believers also should be careful not to add to their troubles by inviting the punishment of God. A restless and complaining spirit is the spirit of Satan. He was the first to rebel, the first to complain, the first to be cursed by God. All rebellion is cursed, and Christians should take very seriously what the Bible says about complaining.

For the last thing we can say about complaining is that God may withdraw his care and protection from those who complain about him. A discontented employee may be sacked and sent to look for another job; and God may send his people to look for another master if they complain about the way he treats them. This might be because he wants to discipline them, and make them trust him, or it might be because they were never true believers at all.

Complaining is bad for you: it is the first step on a slippery downhill road. Some of the Israelites who complained in the wilderness never saw the promised land.

7.
Time to stop complaining

Complaining is always wrong and foolish; but there are some situations in which it is particularly serious. In this chapter we will look at four of these.

First, complaining is particularly serious when we have been greatly blessed. For example; if there are problems in our church life, we are tempted to complain, and to forget how thankful we should be that we are free to worship and evangelise as we wish: in some countries Christians are in fear of losing their freedom or their lives because they belong to Christ. Or if God is good to another church, we are tempted to be jealous and to complain, and to forget how thankful we should be that God has blessed both them and us, although in different ways. Perhaps our turn will come next: if God can do it for them, he can do it for us. Or if God is good to our church at a time when we are having personal problems, we are tempted to forget that we should be thankful for what God is doing, and not complaining about our own personal difficulties. We should always be able to rejoice when God is good to his church.

Second, complaining is particularly serious if we are complaining about trivial things. It would be foolish for a mother to worry because her healthy, happy child had a very slight birthmark. It was wrong of King Ahab, who had control of a whole kingdom, to sulk because he did not own one particular vineyard. And it is stupid for Christians to complain about trivial things.

Third, complaining is particularly serious if it is done by those to whom God has been especially gracious. If a traveller is given free hospitality and finds fault with it, he is rude and ungrateful. Now believers are travellers through this world, and all they have has been given freely to them by God. If God has been that good to them, they have no excuse for complaining.

Finally, complaining is particularly serious if our troubles are part of God's plans to humble us. The Bible says that Enoch walked with God, that is, he saw what God was doing in his life, and submitted to it, and organised his life accordingly. Even in times of trouble Christians are prepared to submit to what God wants, and to accept that he is doing it to humble them and do them spiritual good. It is wrong to complain because God is doing us good; it is especially wrong to go on complaining if he goes on doing us good. Of course, trouble is not easy to bear, but the Bible tells us that later on "it produces a harvest of righteousness and peace for those who have been trained by it" (Hebrews 12:11).

The more that Christians experience the humbling hand of God, the more they should come to appreciate his care of them.

When we find ourselves complaining in one of these situations, it is time to stop. But look again at the third and fourth situations I have described. Christians are always in the position of those to whom God has been especially gracious; Christians are always in the position of those with whom God is dealing for their own good; so complaining is always serious when a Christian does it. And that means that the time to stop complaining is always the same - it is now!

8.
No excuses!

Ever since the Lord questioned Adam and Eve about the first sin, men and women have made excuses for their behaviour. Here are some of the excuses they make for complaining.

"I'm not complaining: I'm just stating facts." It is of course good for believers to look at their situation realistically; but they should not complain. On the contrary, to be aware of the facts is to be aware how great is God's mercy to them. If they are thinking more about their problems than about God's mercies, they have a distorted view of the facts. Being aware of the facts does not stop a Christian from serving God as he ought; but complaining about his problem does. By all means let us face the facts, but that should lead us to be thankful to God, not only for what he has done for us, but for what he has done for others. If we envy them, it shows that we are thinking too much about our troubles, and not enough about the goodness of God.

"I'm not complaining: I'm just conscious of sin." This is easy to say, but very often if the cause of trouble is taken away, the supposed sense of sin vanishes, and that only goes to show there was no real conviction of sin at all. Christians who are really concerned about sin will not want to add to their guilt by complaining; rather, they will be happy to submit to God's discipline.

"I'm unhappy because I do not feel God is with me." But just because we are suffering, it does not mean that God has left us; a father has not turned against his son because he has had occasion to discipline him. God has promised to be with his people, especially in times of trouble: "When you pass through the waters, I will be with you; and when you pass through the rivers, they will not overflow you" (Isaiah 43:2). So God is there, but perhaps believers do not feel it because their complaining spirit has driven away any sense of God's presence: if they want to feel him close they must be quiet and submissive, and must be careful to be the kind of people he wants them to be.

"It's not the suffering, but the attitude of other people that I can't bear." Even the attitude of other people is in God's hands; even wicked people can be used for his purposes, though Christians should remember that wicked people are under the judgement of God, and should pray for them neverthless. However harsh the treatment from other people, Christians should always remember that God is always good to his children. They should praise him: there is no excuse for complaining.

"I never expected this." Christians should expect to have problems in this life, and should prepare for times of trouble, so that when they come they will be ready to face them. And how often are they able to say "I never expected this", when God has been especially good to them!

"My problem is worse than anyone else's." How do you know that? Perhaps your complaining has led you to exaggerate. But if it is true, it means that God has given you a greater opportunity to glorify him than he has given to others. When they see how you cope with your big problem, they will praise God, and perhaps be helped to cope with their little ones.

"My problem prevents me serving God." It sometimes happens that Christians are unable to serve God as they wish because of their circumstances. Of course it is good to want to serve God, and it is natural to grieve when we cannot do so. But this is no excuse for complaining. We are members of the body of Christ. It is better to be an unimportant member of the body of Christ than to be an important person, but a non-member. All Christians have a spiritual calling to fulfil, however insignificant they may think they are. God is better pleased with the simplest acts of the humblest believer than with all the famous deeds of history. What he requires is not fame or brilliant achievements, but faithfulness and patience. Those who display such spiritual qualities will be rewarded in heaven. When humble believers see that, they realise they have no grounds for complaining.

"I cannot bear my circumstances, because they are always unsettled." Perhaps if our circumstances are unsettled it is to teach us to trust God for every step of the way. In any case, our spiritual state is settled, and our eternal good secured. In the meantime, Christ grants us very many blessings: "From the fulness of his grace we have all received one blessing after another" (John 1:16).

"Once I was rich but now I'm poor." That is no excuse for complaining. Can you not be thankful that you were once rich, and had the opportunity to prepare for this time of poverty? Or that you were healthy, and had the opportunity to prepare for this time of sickness? Or free, and had the opportunity to prepare for this time of persecution? A wise sailor uses the calm days to prepare his ship to face the storm. God is not bound to give believers anything, and they should be thankful for every undeserved blessing, past and present. Is it fair to complain about a few difficulties on an otherwise satisfactory journey? But perhaps what this excuse really means is: "I took great pains to get this, and it is not fair that I should lose it." But before Christians take great trouble over anything, they should make sure that they have the right attitude towards it. They must be willing to give it up if something else, something more honouring to God, is what is really best for them.

Questions to help you think about chapters 6-8

1. Look at Philippians 2:14,15. Do we really believe that complaining is a sin?

2. Look at Isaiah 53:3-7. Our Lord Jesus did not complain even when he was cruelly and unjustly crucified. In what way should the character and behaviour of Christ affect that of the Christian?

3. Look at Philippians 4:6,7 and compare 1 Thessalonians 5:16-18. What is the relationship between prayer and Christian contentment?

4. The Israelites whom God brought out of Egypt continually complained against him, and God was angry with them and judged them. Do you think that God is angry with us when we complain about things? Could some of our troubles be God's judgement upon us, as a complaining people?

5. Look at Hebrews 12:7-11. How is trouble and difficulty part of our training in righteousness? What kind of attitude is required of us for such training to prove successful?

6. In what ways do you seek to excuse your complaints?

7. What have you learnt about yourself from this study?

9.
Happiness - how to get it

Christian happiness, or contentment, is the exact opposite of a complaining spirit. It begins within the hearts of believers. It is not possible to steady a ship at sea by propping it up from outside: it must be properly ballasted within. Similarly, there is nothing outside of the Christian which can keep him constantly happy: there needs to be grace within. But if Christians have this grace within, there are certain practical steps they can take to help them get true happiness.

First, they must be careful not to become over-involved with the business of this world. Of course, they cannot live in the world without being to some extent involved in it; and God may lead them to be particularly involved in some aspect of this world's business. But if Christians are to experience true happiness, they must keep to a minimum their involvement with this world's affairs.

Second, they must obey the Word of God as revealed

in the Bible. This should not be difficult to do. The Bible clearly teaches that God works all things together for the good of believers (Romans 8:28); so in serving God they are serving a master who always has their best interests at heart. Believers can happily submit to God's will when they understand this.

Third, like the people mentioned in Hebrews 11, they should live by faith, using their faith to understand or to accept their circumstances. They must have faith not just in the promises of God, but in God himself. He cares for them so well that they do not need to be anxious about anything. Even Socrates, a pagan philosopher, (469-399BC) said, "Since God is so careful for you, why do you need to be careful for anything yourselves?" In times of difficulty, believers should cast their burdens on God, and commit their ways to him. Believing in God will then bring them peace and happiness.

Fourth, they should work hard to be spiritually-minded, to "set their hearts on things above, where Christ is seated at the right hand of God" (Colossians 3:1). If Christians spend little or no time thinking about heavenly things, and a great deal of time brooding over what they want, they only make themselves unhappy. If their minds are set on heavenly things, and they spend time in communion with God, they will not become downcast when they have problems with earthly things.

Closely linked with this is a fifth thing, namely, that Christians should not expect this satisfaction to come from a multitude of earthly things. Paul wrote "If we have food and clothing we will be content with that" (1 Timothy 6:8). People who expect great things are often disappointed. Christians should therefore be content with what they have. They should follow the advice given to Baruch: "Should you then seek great things for yourself? Seek them not" (Jeremiah 45:5). If they expect great spiritual things, they will not be disappointed.

Sixth, they should be dead to the world. Paul wrote "I die daily." Believers know that their only real source of happiness is to be found in spiritual things, and there is a kind of deadness to the things of this world, which "grow strangely dim in the light of God's glory and grace."

Seventh, they should not dwell on their troubles. A sick child scratches his spots which makes it more difficult for them to heal. Christians can get like this with their problems. They talk about them constantly, and they let them eat up their times of prayer. They begin to feel even worse because the problems start to look bigger than they really are. How much better to think about how good God has been, until there is no time left for complaining and unhappiness. When Jacob's wife died in childbirth, she called the boy Benoni, which means "son of my sorrow". Jacob did not wish, however, to be constantly reminded that this boy was the cause of so much sorrow, so he called the boy Benjamin, "son of my right hand". This positive attitude is always helpful for believers to find real happiness.

So, eighth, they should make an effort to think positively about God's dealings with them. It would be a poor friend who constantly misinterpreted his friend's actions, and attributed all sorts of unworthy motives to him. In the same way, it is wrong for believers to misinterpret God's dealings with them. They should think positively about what he does, reasoning, for example, "God saw the danger of my becoming too fond of that, and so he kindly took it away", or "God saw that if he left me a rich man I should fall into sin, and so he kindly made me poorer", or "God is preparing me for some particular task he has in mind, and I am pleased because of that." "Love does not delight in evil" (1 Corinthians 13:6). If you love someone you interpret their actions in a charitable way; and if there are nine bad interpretations and one good one of God's dealings with you, take the one and forget the nine.

Ninth, they should not put too much store by the opinions of other people. For example, Christians may feel perfectly happy until their calm is disturbed by being told that they lack something. But if they were satisfied before being spoken to, why should they let non-christian ideas of happiness upset them? True Christian happiness does not depend on what other people say.

How are Christians to get happiness? All these things can be summed up like this: Christians must not be taken up with the comforts this world offers. Then they will not be so distressed if these things - their property, their families, their reputations, and so on - are taken away.

10.
Happiness - how to keep it

The time of suffering comes: how are believers to remain happy? In this last chapter we will consider five thoughts that will help them to remain happy in times of trouble.

First, troubled Christians should remember how great are the things that God has given them and how insignificant the things they lack. They are tempted to long for the things non-christians have so much of; and this can make them discontented even though they enjoy spiritual privileges unknown to unbelievers. God has given them "every spiritual blessing in Christ" (Ephesians 1:3), and it is therefore wrong for them to become unhappy because they lack things which are earthly and therefore temporary.

Second, troubled Christians should remember the blessings they received in the past. A person who has reached the age of fifty and has suffered two years of illness would do better to thank God for the forty-eight years of perfect health than to start complaining about the two years of illness.

Third, troubled Christians should remember that life in this world is short, whereas eternity is long. Their troubles will soon be over. The Bible tells us "our light and momentary troubles are achieving for us an eternal glory that far outweighs them all. So we fix our eyes not on what is seen, but on what is unseen. For what is seen is temporary, but what is unseen is eternal" (2 Corinthians 4:17,18).

Fourth, troubled Christians should remember that God's people have suffered far worse trials. Jacob was the heir of Abraham and Isaac, but he had to be content to work for his uncle for many years. Moses, who had once lived in the palace of the king of Egypt, spent forty years working as a shepherd, and eventually returned to Egypt so poor that he could get his family and possessions on one donkey (Exodus 4:20). Elijah had to stay in hiding and be fed by ravens. Jeremiah was thrown into a pit. The reformer Martin Luther had nothing to leave his wife and children. And will believers today dare to expect to be exempted from suffering, in a way not granted to these great men of God? Above all, their great example in this, as in all things, is the Lord Jesus Christ, who was worse off than the foxes and the birds, and had nowhere to lay his head.

Finally, troubled Christians should make an effort to praise God for what he has given to them. They have new, spiritual natures: they can praise God in ways that are truly pleasing to him. And they will find that there is real happiness to be had from doing so.

So this is happiness. Have we got it? The Word of God shows us how. Have we started along that route yet? It is easier to talk about happiness than to find it. So young Christians should make an effort to cultivate a quiet, contented spirit from the start of their Christian lives; older Christians should realise how much they have yet to learn; for no true Christian can be satisfied until they have found the real happiness that God gives.

Questions to help you think about chapters 9,10

1. Chapter 9 reminds us that a contented spirit is the work of God's grace in the heart. Does this mean that if we lack a contented spirit it is God's fault? May we continue to grumble and complain until God makes us different?

2. One of the ways in which we learn to be content is by not becoming over-involved in the things of this world (see Matthew 6:19-34 and Colossians 3:1-4). But Christians do have to live in the world and we do have many earthly responsibilities - to our families, to our employers, etc. In the light of this, what in practical terms is meant by not being "over-involved in the business of this world"?

3. Look at Acts 16:16-25. Try to imagine yourself in the place of Paul and Slias and imagine what it must have felt like to be beaten and imprisoned for doing good. How are prayer and praise important to the preserving of a contented spirit in time of trouble?

4. When you have gone through times of trouble, what has helped you to remain content?

5. When other Christians are going through times of trial, how can we best help them to remain content with God and with his dealings with them?

6. What have you learnt from this book? What difference is it going to make to your life?

Other titles in this series of
Great Christian Classics
in easier-to-read and abridged
versions distributed by:

The Evangelical Press,
16/18 High Street,
Welwyn,
Herts, AL6 9EQ,
U.K.

Great Christian Classics series

1. Life by his death
John Owen's "The death of Death in the death of Christ"

2. God willing
John Flavel's "Divine conduct, or The mystery of providence"

3. Biblical Christianity
John Calvin's "The institutes of the Christian religion", Books
I,II,III

4. By God's grace alone
Abraham Booth's "Reign of grace"

5. Born slaves
Martin Luther's "The bondage of the will"

6. The glory of Christ
John Owen's "Meditations on the glory of Christ"

7. Christians are for ever!
John Owen's "The doctrine of the saints' perserverance explained
and confirmed"

A catalogue is available of the other titles published by GPT at:
Grace Publications Trust,
139 Grosvenor Avenue,
London, N5 2NH